A DOCTOR'S TOOLS

A DOCTOR'S TOOLS

Kenny DeSantis

Photographs by

Patricia A. Agre

Introduction by Dr. Fred Agre

DODD, MEAD & COMPANY • New York

Acknowledgments

Special thanks to Candace Erickson, M.D., Director
of Behavioral and Developmental Pediatrics,
Columbia University College of Physicians and
Surgeons; Patty Chadwick, person extraordinaire;
Claudia Palmer, friend and R.N.; Betty Osman,
PhD., and then some; and the DeSantis menage.

Distributed in Canada by
McClelland and Stewart Limited, Toronto
Manufactured in the United States of America

2   3   4   5   6   7   8   9   10

Library of Congress Cataloging in Publication Data

DeSantis, Kenny.
    A doctor's tools.

    Summary: Identifies common doctor's tools such as the
stethoscope, blood pressure cuff, and thermometer,
and describes how they are used and what they feel like.
    1. Medical instruments and apparatus — Juvenile
literature. [1. Medical instruments and apparatus.
2. Medical care]   I. Agre, Patricia, ill.   II. Title.
R856.2.D47 1985   610'.28   85-7026
ISBN 0-396-08516-4
ISBN 0-396-08739-6 (pbk.)

To Fred A.,
Fred B.,
Kenny,
Judy,
Annette,
and
Mrs. Jacovitz

CONTENTS

INTRODUCTION

A visit to the doctor is a frequent occurrence in early childhood. It is often an anxiety-provoking experience. This book, with its illustrations and its descriptive text, should help parents to allay their child's apprehensiveness.

Although many children have "Doctor's Kits," and like to play doctor, when faced with a physician with tools in hand, they readily forget the enjoyment of the previous role playing and revert to being anxious.

I envision that reading and looking at this book, prior, during, and after a visit to the doctor, should help convert the child's experience into a more comfortable event. It is a book that can easily be shared by parent and child, and enjoyed by the child alone.

Fred Agre, M.D., *Associate Professor of Pediatrics, Columbia University College of Physicians and Surgeons*

CHILDREN'S INTRODUCTION

In a doctor's office there are lots of tools. These tools are there to help the doctor take good care of you.

Sometimes you may want to know "What is that? What's it for? How will it feel?"

We hope this book will help to answer some of those questions.

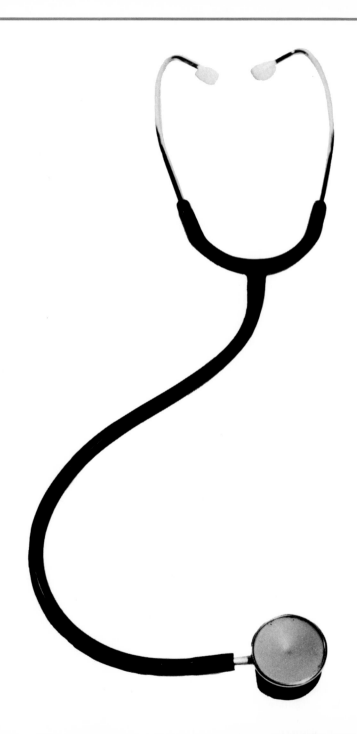

STETHOSCOPE

(STETH-O-SCOPE)

A doctor always has a stethoscope. It is for listening to sounds inside your body.

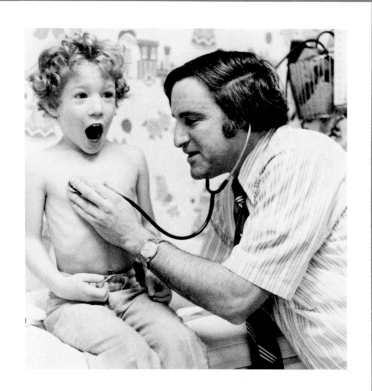

When he puts the plugs in his ears and holds the little round part on your chest, he can hear your heart beat. When he holds it on your back, he can hear the air going in and out of your lungs as you breathe.

Sometimes the little round part of the stethoscope is cold when it touches you.

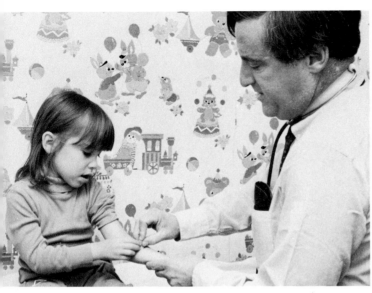

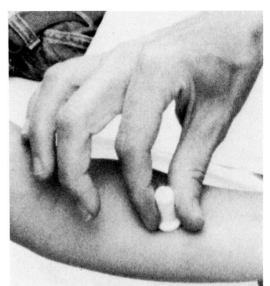

TINE TEST

The tine test is given to see if your lungs are healthy.

When the doctor presses the tool against the skin on the inside of your arm, it feels like a mosquito bite.

After two days, someone in your family will check the spot on your arm to see if there are any little red bumps.

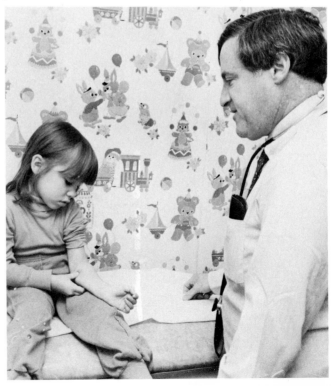

OTOSCOPE

(O-TOE-SCOPE)

An otoscope is used for looking inside your ears.

The tiny, strong light in this tool lets the doctor see if everything is all right. If you have an earache, the doctor can usually see where the trouble is. This doesn't hurt unless you have a very sore ear.

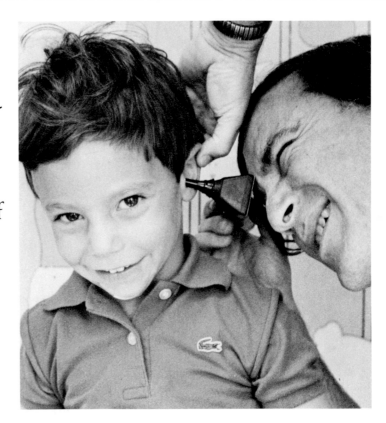

17

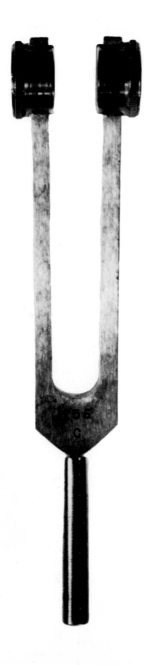

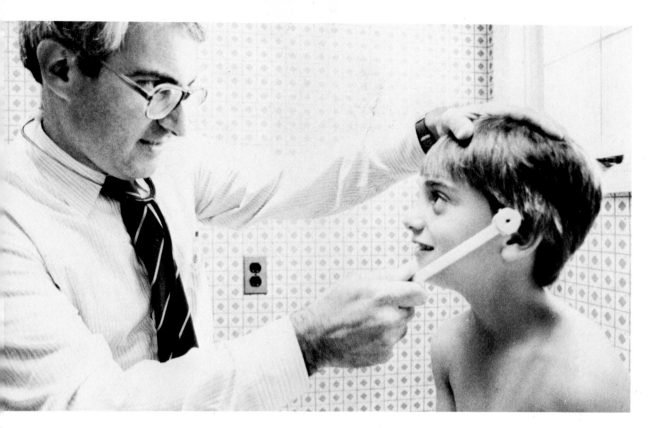

TUNING FORK

With a tuning fork, the doctor tests how well you can hear.

The doctor taps the tuning fork to make it hum. He touches it to your forehead and behind your ear. Then he moves it to the side of your ear. Each time you tell him when the humming sound stops. This is how the doctor can tell if your hearing is all right.

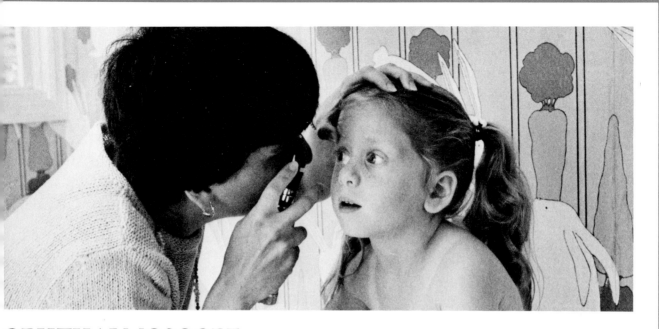

OPHTHALMOSCOPE

(OP-<u>THAL</u>-MO-SCOPE)

This is a special kind of flashlight for examining your eyes.

With the help of the small, bright light in this tool, the doctor can see inside your eyes. He holds the ophthalmoscope very close to your eye, but it doesn't touch you.

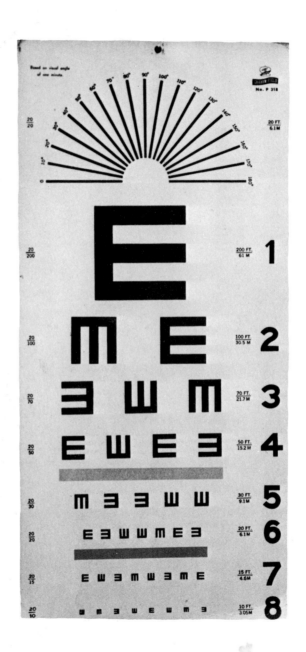

22

EYE CHART

An eye chart shows the doctor how well you can see. It is not a test of how well you can read.

You stand at a place away from the chart, and cover one eye at a time. The doctor points to different "E"s on the chart, and you point in the direction they are going.

The "E"s in the top rows are big and usually easy to see. But they get smaller toward the bottom of the chart. Don't be worried if you can't see all the letters. Very few people can.

TONGUE DEPRESSOR

A doctor uses a tongue depressor to look at your throat. He presses your tongue flat so that he can see into the back of your throat.

The used tongue depressor is thrown away. If you ask for it, the doctor will give you a new one.

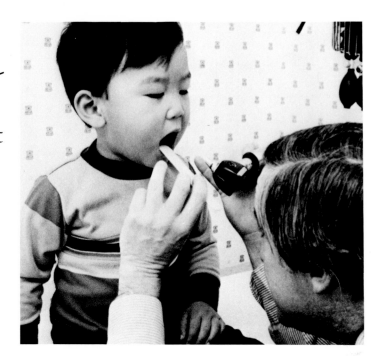

SWAB AND CULTURE PLATE

If you have a sore throat, the doctor or his nurse may take a sample of the germs from your throat.

You open your mouth wide. She rubs the back of your throat gently with the swab. You may feel like gagging, but if you say "ah," that probably won't happen.

The swab is rubbed on the culture plate. Germs from your throat will grow on the culture. In a day or two, the doctor can tell what kind of germs caused your sore throat. He can then decide if you need medicine to make you feel better.

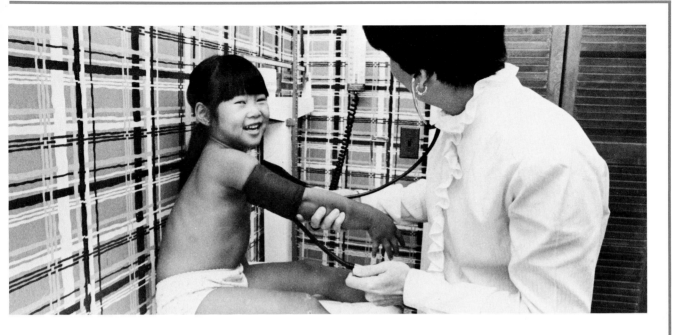

BLOOD PRESSURE CUFF

This tool is used to find out how well your heart is sending blood through your body.

The doctor wraps the cloth cuff around your arm. As she pumps the rubber bulb, the silver line on the gauge goes up, and the cuff gets tighter.

It feels like someone is giving your arm a big hug.

When she stops pumping, she listens with her stethoscope. What she hears is the sound of your blood as it goes through the artery in your arm. While she is listening, the cuff gets looser, and the silver line on the gauge comes down.

BLOOD LANCET

To test your blood, the doctor needs a drop from your finger. He gets this by using a blood lancet.

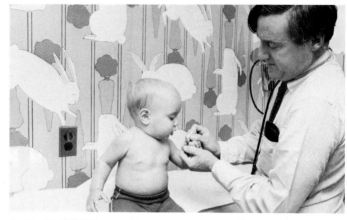

He cleans your finger, and holds the end firmly until it gets slightly numb. Then he pricks your finger with the lancet. It feels like a pinprick. It is a fast, surprise kind of hurt. You hardly have time to say "ouch."

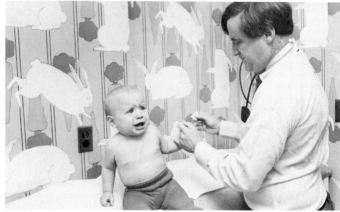

The doctor presses a drop of blood on a glass slide so it can be tested. Then he cleans your finger and puts a Band-Aid on it.

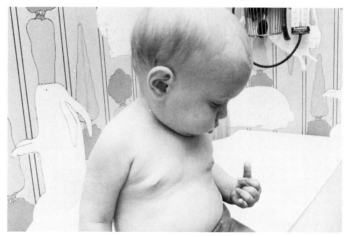

URINE CUP AND DIPSTICK

When you visit the doctor, he may ask you to urinate in a small plastic urine cup. The doctor will then test the sample with a dipstick.

The patches on the dipstick change color when dipped in the urine. The doctor compares the color to a chart to find out if everything is all right.

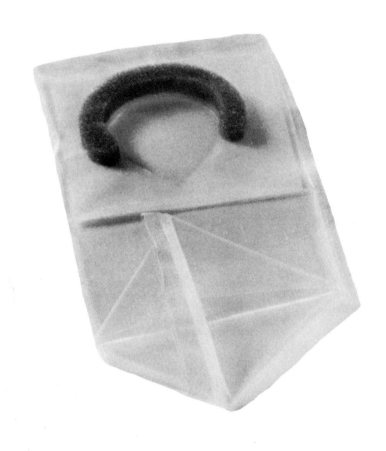

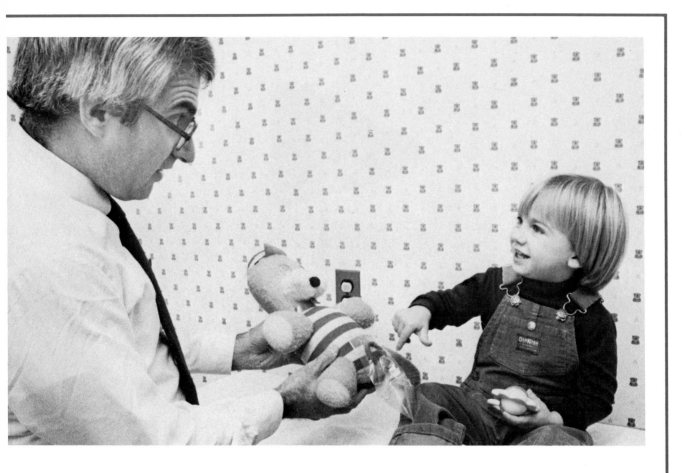

URINE BAG

If you are too young to use a urine cup, the doctor will put a urine bag on you. Sticky adhesive makes it stay on your skin. The urine will go right into the bag.

The doctor then gently removes the bag and tests the urine.

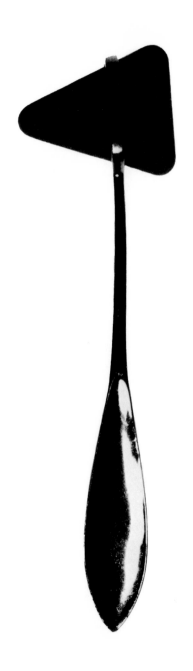

REFLEX HAMMER

This hammer is used for testing nerves in your body.

The doctor lightly taps your knee. When he does this, your foot jumps out all by itself. The nerves in your body make that happen. You don't even have to think about it. This movement is called a reflex action.

The doctor may tap your ankle or elbow, too, to see if they will jump the same way.

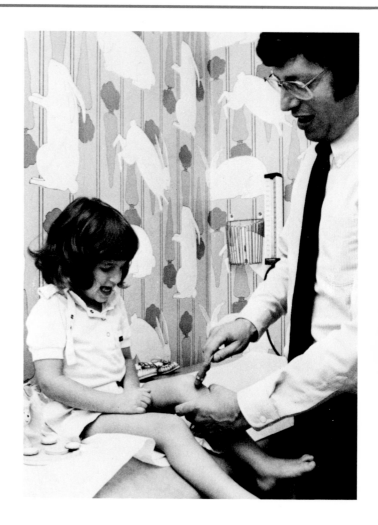

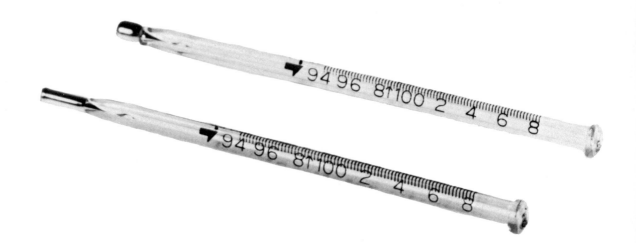

THERMOMETERS

When a doctor wants to know how warm the inside of your body is, he uses a thermometer to take your temperature.

He may use an oral thermometer. It is put in your mouth, under your tongue, for a few minutes. Sometimes it is put under your arm, with your arm held close to your side.

To find out *exactly* how warm you are, the doctor uses a rectal thermometer. He puts ointment on it, so that it slides into your rectum easily. This may be a bit uncomfortable, but it won't hurt.

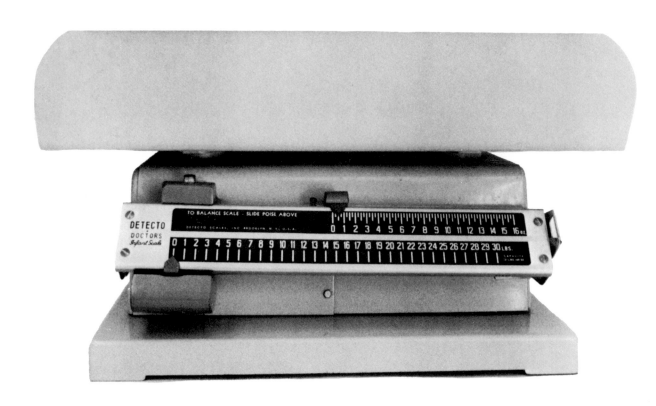

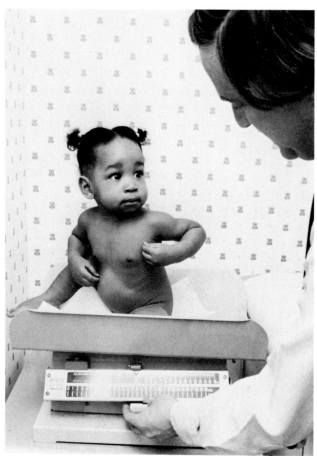

SCALES

To find out how much you weigh, a doctor puts you on a scale. This is one way a doctor can tell how much you have grown.

Babies lie or sit on a scale, while bigger children use a stand-up scale. Scales are sometimes a bit wobbly, so you should hold still.

41

Baby's Own
TAPE MEASURE
INCHES
1 2 3 4 5 6 7
cm.
1 2 3 4 5 6 7 8 9 10 11 12 13 14 15 16 17 18 19 20

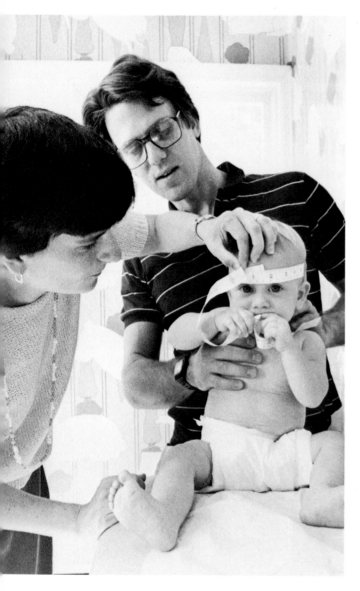

MEASURING TOOLS

A doctor finds out how big and tall you are with a tape measure and a measuring rod.

Babies are measured lying down. The tape measure is stretched from their heads to their heels. Sometimes the doctor measures the baby's head to see how big around it is.

Bigger children stand on a scale that has a measuring rod. The top of the rod is put level with the top of your head. The doctor can then see how many inches you have grown.

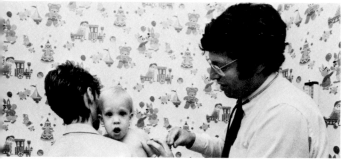

SYRINGE

A syringe is used for giving an injection or shot. This puts medicine into your body quickly.

When the doctor sticks the end of the needle under your skin and pushes the plunger, it will sting or pinch. It's all right to say "ouch," because it does hurt. The place where you get a shot may be sore for a day or two.

You get shots to help keep you from getting sick, or to make you better if you are already sick.

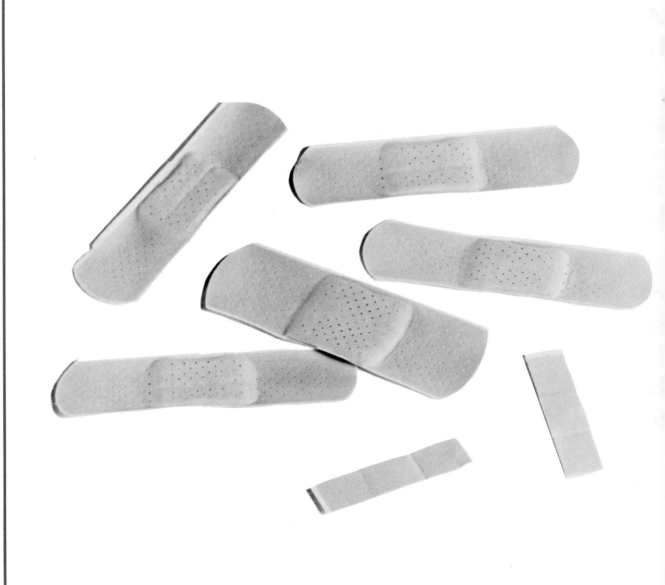

BAND-AID

A doctor's tool that you use at home, too, is a Band-Aid.

Sometimes the doctor puts a Band-Aid on the place where you get a shot. The Band-Aid protects it and keeps it clean.

At home, you use a Band-Aid when you cut yourself or scrape your knee to protect it. Not having to see where you hurt yourself can make you feel better, too.

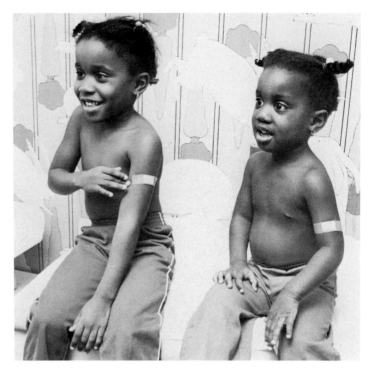